I LOVE YOU

I LOVE YOU

An Anthology of Love Poems

Compiled by
GERRISH GRAY

TIGER OF THE STRIPE ♥ RICHMOND

Paperback first published in 2009 by
TIGER OF THE STRIPE
50 Albert Road
Richmond
Surrey TW10 6DP
United Kingdom

© Gerrish Gray 2007
All rights reserved

ISBN 978-1-904799-35-1

Typeset in the UK by
Tiger of the Stripe

Printed and bound
in the UK and USA by
by Lightning Source

Contents

There is a Lady Sweet and Kind ANONYMOUS 7
From a Lady to a Gentleman, in Answer to a Complimentary Copy of Verses ANONYMOUS 8
A Cheerful Tempered Lover's Farewell to His Mistress JOANNA BAILLIE 10
A Sonnet FRANCIS BEAUMONT 12
Song APHRA BEHN 14
The One Before the Last RUPERT BROOKE 76
Memory WILLIAM BROWNE OF TAVISTOCK 17
Song WILLIAM BROWNE OF TAVISTOCK 18
How Do I Love Thee? ELIZABETH BARRETT BROWNING 19
Love in life ROBERT BROWNING 20
My Bonnie Mary ROBERT BURNS 21
A Red, Red Rose ROBERT BURNS 22
So We'll Go No More a-Roving LORD BYRON 23
She Walks in Beauty LORD BYRON 24
Cherry-Ripe THOMAS CAMPION 25
The Unfading Beauty THOMAS CAREW 26
Ask me, Lesbia CATULLUS 27
'Why Do I love' You, Sir? EMILY DICKINSON 28
The Good Morrow JOHN DONNE 29
The Sun Rising JOHN DONNE 30
Song JOHN DONNE 32
The Triple Fool JOHN DONNE 34
To His Coy Love MICHAEL DRAYTON 35
How Many Paltry Foolish Painted Things MICHAEL DRAYTON 36
To One that Asked Me Why I Loved J. G. EPHELIA [LADY MARY VILLIERS] 37
To Plead My Faith ROBERT DEVEREUX, EARL OF ESSEX 38
To a Lady Asking Him How Long He Would Love Her SIR GEORGE ETHEREGE 39
Beauty Clear and Fair JOHN FLETCHER 40
Wooing Song GILES FLETCHER 41
Why, My Heart W. E. HENLEY 43
To Anthea, Who May Command Him Anything ROBERT HERRICK 44
The Night-Piece: To Julia ROBERT HERRICK 45
To Electra ROBERT HERRICK 46
Time of Roses THOMAS HOOD 47
Jenny Kiss'd Me LEIGH HUNT 48
To Celia BEN JONSON 49
Cards and Kisses JOHN LYLY 50
Rosaline THOMAS LODGE 51

To Amarantha; That She Would Dishevel Her Hair
  RICHARD LOVELACE 53
To Lucasta, Going to the Wars RICHARD LOVELACE 55
The Scrutiny RICHARD LOVELACE 56
Love Unkind ISABEL ECCLESTONE MACKAY 57
The Passionate Shepherd to His Love CHRISTOPHER MARLOWE 58
To His Coy Mistress ANDREW MARVELL 59
I'll Never Love Thee More JAMES GRAHAM 61
Beauty Bathing ANTHONY MUNDAY 63
I Do Not Love Thee CAROLINE NORTON 64
Rondel CHARLES D'ORLEANS 65
A Love Symphony A. W. E. O'SHAUGHNESSY 66
The Enchantment THOMAS OTWAY 67
What Cunning Can Express EDWARD DE VERE 68
Love and Age THOMAS LOVE PEACOCK 70
Phillida and Coridon NICHOLAS BRETON 72
The Nymph's Reply to the Shepherd SIR WALTER RALEIGH 73
The Ripest Peach JAMES WHITCOMB RILEY 74
A Song of a Young Lady to Her Ancient Lover JOHN WILMOT 75
Love from the North CHRISTINA ROSSETTI 76
Phyllis is My Only Joy SIR CHARLES SEDLEY 78
To Celia SIR CHARLES SEDLEY 79
Sonnet XVIII WILLIAM SHAKESPEARE 80
Sonnet LVII WILLIAM SHAKESPEARE 81
Sonnet LXXV WILLIAM SHAKESPEARE 82
Sonnet CXXX WILLIAM SHAKESPEARE 83
Sonnet XCI WILLIAM SHAKESPEARE 84
Sonnet CXLI WILLIAM SHAKESPEARE 85
The Indian Serenade PERCY BYSSHE SHELLEY 86
Love's Arithmetic SIR EDWARD SHERBURNE 87
Had I a Heart for Falsehood Framed RICHARD BRINSLEY SHERIDAN 88
Cupid, Because Thou SIR PHILIP SIDNEY 89
I Prithee Send Me Back My Heart SIR JOHN SUCKLING 90
Out Upon It, I Have Lov'd SIR JOHN SUCKLING 91
When, Dearest, I but Think of Thee SIR JOHN SUCKLING 92
Tides SARA TEASDALE 93
Arbor Amoris FRANÇOIS VILLON 94
Go, Lovely Rose EDMUND WALLER 96
To Phyllis EDMUND WALLER 97
The Self Banished EDMUND WALLER 98
Against Indifference CHARLES WEBBE 99
The Je Ne Scai Quoi WILLIAM WHITEHEAD 100
I Loved a Lass GEORGE WITHER 101
A Complaint WILLIAM WORDSWORTH 103
Rondeau SIR THOMAS WYATT 104
Sonnet SIR THOMAS WYATT 105

There is a Lady Sweet and Kind

ANONYMOUS

There is a Lady sweet and kind,
Was never face so pleased my mind;
I did but see her passing by,
And yet I love her till I die.
Her gesture, motion, and her smiles,
Her wit, her voice my heart beguiles,
Beguiles my heart, I know not why,
And yet I love her till I die.
Cupid is winged and doth range,
Her country so my love doth change:
But change she earth, or change she sky,
Yet will I love her till I die.

From a Lady to a Gentleman, in Answer to a Complimentary Copy of Verses

ANONYMOUS

Your lines poetic, Sir, I read,
This morning, when I rose from bed;
The air was chill, and far as sight
The hills and fields were clad in white.
The sun, tho' finish'd half his race,
In clouds envelop'd, hid his face;
And far and wide the naked plain,
Confest stern winter's tyrant reign.
But yet you say, 'whene'er my eyes,
With winning smiles, salute the skies,

The clouds disperse; unseen before,
Phoebus conceals his face no more.
Whene'er I trip along the fields,
The spring her choicest tribute yields;
The flow'rs, spontaneous, at my feet,
Adorn my path, o'erspread my seat.'

Prone to believe that I possest
Virtues superior to the rest,
Myself I thought another creature.
More beauties spy'd in ev'ry feature.

To my weak sex, elate with pride,
I scarce could think myself ally'd;
I drest, in short, and out I went,
To try the fond experiment.

My first essay was on the plain—
I tript—return'd—and tript again;
But still no flowers beneath my feet
Spontaneous sprang, nor deckt my seat.
The next, to make the storms subside,
My influence on the skies I try'd;

To heav'n my eyes I gently rais'd,
And form'd the smile that Damon prais'd.
Their softest smile my features wore,
But all continued as before;
Till strange to tell! a show'r of rain
Th'unpolish'd clouds return'd again.
So home return'd chagrin'd and sad,
Convinc'd that you was fool—or mad.

A Cheerful Tempered Lover's Farewell to His Mistress

JOANNA BAILLIE

The light winds on the streamers play
That soon shall bear me far away;
My comrades give the parting cheer,
And I alone have linger'd here.
Now Phill, my love, since it will be,
And I must bid farewell to thee,
Since ev'ry hope of thee is flown,
Ne'er send me from thee with a frown;
But let me kindly take thy hand,
And bid God bless me in a foreign land.

No more I'll loiter by thy side,
Well pleas'd thy gamesome taunts to bide;
Nor lovers' gambols lightly try
To make me graceful in thine eye;
Nor sing the merry roundelay,
To cheer thee at the close of day.
Yet ne'ertheless tho' we must part,
I'll bear thee still upon my heart;
And oft I'll fill the ruddy glass,
To toast my lovely scornful lass.
Far hence, upon a foreign shore,
Still will I keep an open door,
And still my little fortune share
With all who ever breath'd my native air.
And who thy beauteous face hath seen,
Or ever near thy dwelling been,
Shall push about the flowing bowl,

And be the matter of the whole.
And ev'ry woman for thy sake,
Though proud and cruel, as they're weak,
Shall in my walls protection find,
Thou fairest of a fickle kind.

O, dearly! dearly! have I paid,
Thou little haughty cruel maid,
To give that inward peace to thee,
Which thou hast ta'en away from me.
Soft hast thou slept, with bosom light,
Whilst I have watch'd the weary night;
And now I cross the surgy deep,
That thou may'st still untroubled sleep—
But in thine eyes, what do I see,
That looks as tho' they pitied me?
I thank thee, Phill, yet be not sad,
I leave no blame upon thy head.
I would, more grac'd with pleasing make,
I had been better for thy sake,
But yet, perhaps, when I shall dwell
Far hence, thou'lt sometimes think how well—
I dare not stay, since we must part,
T'expose a fond and foolish heart;
Where'er I go, it beats for you,
God bless ye, Phill. adieu! adieu!

A Sonnet

FRANCIS BEAUMONT

Flattering Hope, away and leave me,
She'll not come, thou dost deceive me;
Hark the cock crows, th'envious light
Chides away the silent night;
Yet she comes not, oh! how I tire
Betwixt cold fear and hot desire.

Here alone enforced to tarry
While the tedious minutes marry,
And get hours, those days and years,
Which I count with sighs and fears
Yet she comes not, oh! how I tire
Betwixt cold fear and hot desire.

Restless thoughts a while remove
Unto the bosom of my love,
Let her languish in my pain,
Fear and hope, and fear again;
Then let her tell me, in love's fire,
What torment's like unto desire?

Endless wishing, tedious longing,
Hopes and fears together thronging;
Rich in dreams, yet poor in waking,
Let her be in such a taking:
Then let her tell me in love's fire,
What torment's like unto desire?

Come then, Love, prevent day's eyeing,
My desire would fain be dying:
Smother me with breathless kisses,
Let me dream no more of blisses;
But tell me, which is in Love's fire
Best, to enjoy, or to desire?

Song

APHRA BEHN

Love in fantastic triumph sate
  Whilst bleeding hearts around him flow'd,
For whom fresh pains he did create
  And strange tyrannic power he show'd:
From thy bright eyes he took his fires,
  Which round about in sport he hurl'd;
But 'twas from mine he took desires
  Enough t'undo the amorous world.
From me he took his sighs and tears,
  From thee his pride and cruelty;
From me his languishments and fears,
  And every killing dart from thee.
Thus thou and I the god have arm'd
  And set him up a deity;
But my poor heart alone is harm'd,
  Whilst thine the victor is, and free!

The One Before the Last

RUPERT BROOKE

I dreamt I was in love again
  With the One Before the Last,
And smiled to greet the pleasant pain
  Of that innocent young past.

But I jumped to feel how sharp had been
  The pain when it did live,
How the faded dreams of Nineteen-ten
  Were Hell in Nineteen-five.

The boy's woe was as keen and clear,
  The boy's love just as true,
And the One Before the Last, my dear,
  Hurt quite as much as you.

* * * * *

Sickly I pondered how the lover
  Wrongs the unanswering tomb,
And sentimentalizes over
  What earned a better doom.

Gently he tombs the poor dim last time,
  Strews pinkish dust above,
And sighs, 'The dear dead boyish pastime!
  But THIS—ah, God!—is Love!'

—Better oblivion hide dead true loves,
  Better the night enfold,
Than men, to eke the praise of new loves,
  Should lie about the old!

* * * * *

Oh! bitter thoughts I had in plenty.
  But here's the worst of it—
I shall forget, in Nineteen-twenty,
  YOU ever hurt a bit!

Memory

WILLIAM BROWNE OF TAVISTOCK

So shuts the marigold her leaves
   At the departure of the sun;
So from the honeysuckle sheaves
   The bee goes when the day is done;
So sits the turtle when she is but one,
And so all woe, as I since she is gone.

To some few birds kind Nature hath
   Made all the summer as one day:
Which once enjoy'd, cold winter's wrath
   As night they sleeping pass away.
Those happy creatures are, that know not yet
The pain to be deprived or to forget.

I oft have heard men say there be
   Some that with confidence profess
The helpful Art of Memory:
   But could they teach Forgetfulness,
I'd learn; and try what further art could do
To make me love her and forget her too.

Song

WILLIAM BROWNE OF TAVISTOCK

For her gait, if she be walking;
Be she sitting, I desire her
For her state's sake; and admire her
For her wit if she be talking;
   Gait and state and wit approve her;
   For which all and each I love her.

Be she sullen, I commend her
For a modest. Be she merry,
For a kind one her prefer I.
Briefly, everything doth lend her
   So much grace, and so approve her,
   That for everything I love her.

How Do I Love Thee?

ELIZABETH BARRETT BROWNING

How do I love thee? Let me count the ways.
I love thee to the depth and breadth and height
My soul can reach, when feeling out of sight
For the ends of Being and ideal Grace.
I love thee to the level of every day's
Most quiet need, by sun and candlelight.
I love thee freely, as men strive for Right;
I love thee purely, as they turn from Praise.
I love with a passion put to use
In my old griefs, and with my childhood's faith.
I love thee with a love I seemed to lose
With my lost saints, I love thee with the breath,
Smiles, tears, of all my life! and, if God choose,
I shall but love thee better after death.

Love in life

ROBERT BROWNING

I

Room after room,
I hunt the house through
We inhabit together.
Heart, fear nothing, for, heart, thou shalt find her—
Next time, herself!—not the trouble behind her
Left in the curtain, the couch's perfume!
As she brushed it, the cornice-wreath blossomed anew:
Yon looking-glass gleaned at the wave of her feather.

II

Yet the day wears,
And door succeeds door;
I try the fresh fortune—
Range the wide house from the wing to the centre.
Still the same chance! She goes out as I enter.
Spend my whole day in the quest,—who cares?
But 'tis twilight, you see,—with such suites to explore,
Such closets to search, such alcoves to importune!

My Bonnie Mary

ROBERT BURNS

Go fetch to me a pint o' wine,
  An' fill it in a silver tassie,
That I may drink, before I go,
  A service to my bonnie lassie.
The boat rocks at the pier o' Leith,
  Fu' loud the wind blaws frae the ferry,
The ship rides by the Berwick-law,
  And I maun leave my bonnie Mary.

The trumpets sound, the banners fly,
  The glittering spears are ranked ready;
The shouts o' war are heard afar,
  The battle closes thick and bloody;
But it's no the roar o' sea or shore
  Wad mak me langer wish to tarry;
Nor shout o' war that's heard afar—
  It's leaving thee, my bonnie Mary!

A Red, Red Rose

ROBERT BURNS

O my Luve's like a red, red rose
   That's newly sprung in June:
O my Luve's like the melodie
   That's sweetly play'd in tune!

As fair art thou, my bonnie lass,
   So deep in luve am I:
And I will luve thee still, my dear,
   Till a' the seas gang dry:

Till a' the seas gang dry, my dear,
   And the rocks melt wi' the sun;
I will luve thee still, my dear,
   While the sands o' life shall run.

And fare thee weel, my only Luve,
   And fare thee weel a while!
And I will come again, my Luve,
   Tho' it were ten thousand mile.

So We'll Go No More a-Roving

LORD BYRON

So we'll go no more a-roving
So late into the night,
Though the heart still be as loving,
And the moon still be as bright.

For the sword outwears its sheath,
And the soul outwears the breast,
And the heart must pause to breathe,
And love itself have rest.

Though the night was made for loving,
And the day returns too soon,
Yet we'll go no more a-roving
By the light of the moon.

She Walks in Beauty

LORD BYRON

She walks in Beauty, like the night
Of cloudless climes and starry skies;
And all that's best of dark and bright
Meet in her aspect and her eyes:
Thus mellowed to that tender light
Which Heaven to gaudy day denies.
One shade the more, one ray the less,
Had half impaired the nameless grace
Which waves in every raven tress,
Or softly lightens o'er her face;
Where thoughts serenely sweet express,
How pure, how dear their dwelling-place.
And on that cheek, and o'er that brow,
So soft, so calm, yet eloquent,
The smiles that win, the tints that glow,
But tell of days in goodness spent,
A mind at peace with all below,
A heart whose love is innocent!

Cherry-Ripe

THOMAS CAMPION

There is a garden in her face
  Where roses and white lilies blow;
A heavenly paradise is that place,
  Wherein all pleasant fruits do flow:
    There cherries grow which none may buy
    Till 'Cherry-ripe' themselves do cry.
Those cherries fairly do enclose
  Of orient pearl a double row,
Which when her lovely laughter shows,
  They look like rose-buds fill'd with snow;
    Yet them nor peer nor prince can buy
    Till 'Cherry-ripe' themselves do cry.
Her eyes like angels watch them still;
  Her brows like bended bows do stand,
Threat'ning with piercing frowns to kill
  All that attempt with eye or hand
    Those sacred cherries to come nigh,
    Till 'Cherry-ripe' themselves do cry.

The Unfading Beauty

THOMAS CAREW

He that loves a rosy cheek,
  Or a coral lip admires,
Or from star-like eyes doth seek
  Fuel to maintain his fires:
As old Time makes these decay,
So his flames must waste away.
But a smooth and steadfast mind,
  Gentle thoughts and calm desires,
Hearts with equal love combined,
  Kindle never-dying fires.
Where these are not, I despise
Lovely cheeks or lips or eyes.

Ask me, Lesbia

CATULLUS

Ask me, Lesbia, what the sum delightful
Of thy kisses, enough to charm, to tire me?
Multitudinous as the grains on even
Lybian sands aromatic of Cyrene;

'Twixt Jove's oracle in the sandy desert
And where royally Battus old reposeth;
Yea a company vast as in the silence
Stars which stealthily gaze on happy lovers;
E'en so many the kisses I to kiss thee.

Count, wild lover, enough to charm, to tire me;
These no curious eye can wholly number,
Tongue of jealousy ne'er bewitch nor harm them.

'Why Do I love' You, Sir?

EMILY DICKINSON

'Why do I love' You, Sir?
Because—
The Wind does not require the Grass
To answer—Wherefore when He pass
She cannot keep Her place.

Because He knows—and
Do not You—
And We know not—
Enough for Us
The Wisdom it be so—

The Lightning—never asked an Eye
Wherefore it shut—when He was by—
Because He knows it cannot speak—
And reasons not contained—
—Of Talk—
There be—preferred by Daintier Folk—

The Sunrise—Sire—compelleth Me—
Because He's Sunrise—and I see—
Therefore—Then—
I love Thee—

The Good Morrow

JOHN DONNE

I wonder by my troth, what thou and I
Did, till we loved? were we not wean'd till then?
But suck'd on country pleasures, childishly?
Or snorted we in the Seven Sleepers' den?
'Twas so; but this, all pleasures fancies be;
If ever any beauty I did see,
Which I desired, and got, 'twas but a dream of thee.

And now good-morrow to our waking souls,
Which watch not one another out of fear;
For love all love of other sights controls,
And makes one little room an everywhere.
Let sea-discoverers to new worlds have gone;
Let maps to other, worlds on worlds have shown;
Let us possess one world; each hath one, and is one.

My face in thine eye, thine in mine appears,
And true plain hearts do in the faces rest;
Where can we find two better hemispheres
Without sharp north, without declining west?
Whatever dies, was not mix'd equally;
If our two loves be one, or thou and I
Love so alike that none can slacken, none can die.

The Sun Rising

JOHN DONNE

Busy old fool, unruly Sun,
Why dost thou thus,
Through windows, and through curtains, call on us?
Must to thy motions lovers' seasons run?
Saucy pedantic wretch, go chide
Late school-boys and sour prentices,
Go tell court-huntsmen that the king will ride,
Call country ants to harvest offices;
Love, all alike, no season knows nor clime,
Nor hours, days, months, which are the rags of time.

Thy beams so reverend, and strong
Why shouldst thou think?
I could eclipse and cloud them with a wink,
But that I would not lose her sight so long._
If her eyes have not blinded thine,
Look, and to-morrow late tell me,
Whether both th'Indias of spice and mine
Be where thou left'st them, or lie here with me.
Ask for those kings whom thou saw'st yesterday,
And thou shalt hear, 'All here in one bed lay.'

She's all states, and all princes I;
Nothing else is;
Princes do but play us; compared to this,
All honour's mimic, all wealth alchemy.
Thou, Sun, art half as happy as we,
In that the world's contracted thus ;
Thine age asks ease, and since thy duties be
To warm the world, that's done in warming us.
Shine here to us, and thou art everywhere;
This bed thy centre is, these walls thy sphere.

Song

JOHN DONNE

Sweetest love, I do not go,
For weariness of thee,
Nor in hope the world can show
A fitter love for me;
But since that I
At the last must part, 'tis best,
Thus to use myself in jest
By feigned deaths to die.

Yesternight the sun went hence,
And yet is here to-day;
He hath no desire nor sense,
Nor half so short a way;
Then fear not me,
But believe that I shall make
Speedier journeys, since I take
More wings and spurs than he.

O how feeble is man's power,
That if good fortune fall,
Cannot add another hour,
Nor a lost hour recall;
But come bad chance,
And we join to it our strength,
And we teach it art and length,
Itself o'er us to advance.

When thou sigh'st, thou sigh'st not wind,
But sigh'st my soul away;
When thou weep'st, unkindly kind,
My life's blood doth decay.
It cannot be
That thou lovest me as thou say'st,
If in thine my life thou waste,
That art the best of me.

Let not thy divining heart
Forethink me any ill;
Destiny may take thy part,
And may thy fears fulfil.
But think that we
Are but turn'd aside to sleep.
They who one another keep
Alive, ne'er parted be.

The Triple Fool

JOHN DONNE

I am two fools, I know,
For loving, and for saying so
   In whining poetry;
But where's that wise man, that would not be I,
   If she would not deny?
Then as th'earth's inward narrow crooked lanes
   Do purge sea water's fretful salt away,
I thought, if I could draw my pains
   Through rhyme's vexation, I should them allay.
Grief brought to numbers cannot be so fierce,
For he tames it, that fetters it in verse.
   But when I have done so,
   Some man, his art and voice to show,
      Doth set and sing my pain;
And, by delighting many, frees again
   Grief, which verse did restrain.
To love and grief tribute of verse belongs,
   But not of such as pleases when 'tis read.
Both are increasèd by such songs,
   For both their triumphs so are publishèd,
And I, which was two fools, do so grow three.
Who are a little wise, the best fools be.

To His Coy Love

MICHAEL DRAYTON

I pray thee, leave, love me no more,
  Call home the heart you gave me!
I but in vain that saint adore
  That can but will not save me.
These poor half-kisses kill me quite—
  Was ever man thus served?
Amidst an ocean of delight
  For pleasure to be starved?

Show me no more those snowy breasts
  With azure riverets branched,
Where, whilst mine eye with plenty feasts,
  Yet is my thirst not stanched;
O Tantalus, thy pains ne'er tell!
  By me thou art prevented:
'Tis nothing to be plagued in Hell,
  But thus in Heaven tormented.

Clip me no more in those dear arms,
  Nor thy life's comfort call me,
O these are but too powerful charms,
  And do but more enthral me!
But see how patient I am grown
  In all this coil about thee:
Come, nice thing, let my heart alone,
  I cannot live without thee!

How Many Paltry Foolish Painted Things

MICHAEL DRAYTON

How many paltry foolish painted things,
That now in coaches trouble every street,
Shall be forgotten, whom no poet sings,
Ere they be well wrapped in their winding-sheet!
Where I to thee eternity shall give,
When nothing else remaineth of these days,
And queens hereafter shall be glad to live
Upon the alms of thy superfluous praise.
Virgins and matrons, reading these my rhymes,
Shall be so much delighted with thy story
That they shall grieve they lived not in these times,
To have seen thee, their sex's only glory:
So shalt thou fly above the vulgar throng,
Still to survive in my immortal song.

To One that Asked Me Why I Loved J. G.

EPHELIA [LADY MARY VILLIERS]

Why do I love? go ask the glorious sun
Why every day it round the world doth run:
Ask Thames and Tiber why they ebb and flow:
Ask damask roses why in June they blow:
Ask ice and hail the reason why the're cold:
Decaying beauties, why they will grow old:
They'll tell thee Fate, that everything doth move,
Inforces them to this, and me to love.
There is no reason for our love or hate,
'Tis irresistible as Death or Fate;
'Tis not his face; I've sense enough to see
That is not good, though doated on by me:
Nor is't his tongue that has this conquest won,
For that at least is equalled by my own:
His carriage can to none obliging be,
'Tis rude, affected, full of vanity:
Strangely ill natur'd, peevish and unkind,
Unconstant, false, to jealousy inclin'd:
His temper could not have so great a power,
'Tis mutable, and changes every hour:
Those vigorous years that women so adore
Are past in him: he's twice my age and more;
And yet I love this false, this worthless man,
With all the passion that a woman can;
Doat on his imperfections, though I spy
Nothing to love; I love, and know not why.
Since 'tis decreed in the dark book of Fate,
That I should love, and he should be ingrate.

To Plead My Faith

ROBERT DEVEREUX, EARL OF ESSEX

To plead my faith where faith had no reward,
To move remorse where favor is not borne,
To heap complaints where she doth not regard,—
Were fruitless, bootless, vain, and yield but scorn.

I lovéd her whom all the world admired,
I was refused of her that can love none;
And my vain hopes, which far too high aspired,
Is dead, and buried, and for ever gone.

Forget my name, since you have scorned my love,
And woman-like do not too late lament;
Since for your sake I do all mischief prove,
I none accuse nor nothing do repent.

I was as fond as ever she was fair,
Yet loved I not more than I now despair.

To a Lady Asking Him How Long He Would Love Her

SIR GEORGE ETHEREGE

It is not, Celia, in our power
  To say how long our love will last;
It may be we within this hour
  May lose those joys we now do taste;
The Blessed, that immortal be,
From change in love are only free.

Then since we mortal lovers are,
  Ask not how long our love will last;
But while it does, let us take care
  Each minute be with pleasure past:
Were it not madness to deny
To live because we're sure to die?

Beauty Clear and Fair

JOHN FLETCHER

Beauty clear and fair,
  Where the air
Rather like a perfume dwells;
  Where the violet and the rose
  Their blue veins and blush disclose,
And come to honour nothing else:

  Where to live near
  And planted there
Is to live, and still live new;
  Where to gain a favour is
  More than light, perpetual bliss—
Make me live by serving you!

  Dear, again back recall
  To this light,
A stranger to himself and all!
  Both the wonder and the story
  Shall be yours, and eke the glory;
I am your servant, and your thrall.

Wooing Song

GILES FLETCHER

Love is the blossom where there blows
Every thing that lives or grows:
Love doth make the Heav'ns to move,
And the Sun doth burn in love:
Love the strong and weak doth yoke,
And makes the ivy climb the oak,
Under whose shadows lions wild,
Soften'd by love, grow tame and mild:
Love no med'cine can appease,
He burns the fishes in the seas:
Not all the skill his wounds can stench,
Not all the sea his fire can quench.
Love did make the bloody spear
Once a leavy coat to wear,
While in his leaves there shrouded lay
Sweet birds, for love that sing and play
And of all love's joyful flame
I the bud and blossom am.
  Only bend thy knee to me,
  Thy wooing shall thy winning be!

See, see the flowers that below
Now as fresh as morning blow;
And of all the virgin rose
That as bright Aurora shows;
How they all unleaved die,
Losing their virginity!
Like unto a summer shade,
But now born, and now they fade.

Every thing doth pass away;
There is danger in delay:
Come, come, gather then the rose,
Gather it, or it you lose!
All the sand of Tagus' shore
Into my bosom casts his ore:
All the valleys' swimming corn
To my house is yearly borne:
Every grape of every vine
Is gladly bruised to make me wine:
While ten thousand kings, as proud,
To carry up my train have bow'd,
And a world of ladies send me
In my chambers to attend me:
All the stars in Heav'n that shine,
And ten thousand more, are mine:
  Only bend thy knee to me,
  Thy wooing shall thy winning be!

Why, My Heart

W. E. HENLEY

Why, my heart, do we love her so?
(Geraldine, Geraldine!)
Why does the great sea ebb and flow? -
Why does the round world spin?
Geraldine, Geraldine,
Bid me my life renew:
What is it worth unless I win,
Love—love and you?

Why, my heart, when we speak her name
(Geraldine, Geraldine!)
Throbs the word like a flinging flame?—
Why does the Spring begin?
Geraldine, Geraldine,
Bid me indeed to be:
Open your heart, and take us in,
Love—love and me.

To Anthea, Who May Command Him Anything

ROBERT HERRICK

Bid me to live, and I will live
   Thy Protestant to be;
Or bid me love, and I will give
   A loving heart to thee.

A heart as soft, a heart as kind,
   A heart as sound and free
As in the whole world thou canst find,
   That heart I'll give to thee.

Bid that heart stay, and it will stay
   To honour thy decree:
Or bid it languish quite away,
   And 't shall do so for thee.

Bid me to weep, and I will weep
   While I have eyes to see:
And, having none, yet will I keep
   A heart to weep for thee.

Bid me despair, and I'll despair
   Under that cypress-tree:
Or bid me die, and I will dare
   E'en death to die for thee.

Thou art my life, my love my heart,
   The very eyes of me:
And hast command of every part
   To live and die for thee.

The Night-Piece: To Julia

ROBERT HERRICK

Her eyes the glow-worm lend thee,
The shooting stars attend thee;
   And the elves also,
   Whose little eyes glow
Like the sparks of fire, befriend thee.

No Will-o'-the-wisp mislight thee,
Nor snake or slow-worm bite thee;
   But on, on thy way
   Not making a stay,
Since ghost there's none to affright thee.

Let not the dark thee cumber:
What though the moon does slumber?
   The stars of the night
   Will lend thee their light
Like tapers clear without number.

Then, Julia, let me woo thee,
Thus, thus to come unto me;
   And when I shall meet
   Thy silv'ry feet,
My soul I'll pour into thee.

To Electra

ROBERT HERRICK

I dare not ask a kiss,
  I dare not beg a smile,
Lest having that, or this,
  I might grow proud the while.
No, no, the utmost share
  Of my desire shall be
Only to kiss that air
  That lately kissed thee.

Time of Roses

THOMAS HOOD

It was not in the Winter
  Our loving lot was cast;
It was the time of roses—
  We pluck'd them as we pass'd!

That churlish season never frown'd
  On early lovers yet:
O no—the world was newly crown'd
  With flowers when first we met!

'Twas twilight, and I bade you go,
  But still you held me fast;
It was the time of roses—
  We pluck'd them as we pass'd!

Jenny Kiss'd Me

LEIGH HUNT

Jenny kiss'd me when we met,
  Jumping from the chair she sat in;
Time, you thief, who love to get
  Sweets into your list, put that in!
Say I'm weary, say I'm sad,
  Say that health and wealth have miss'd me,
Say I'm growing old, but add,
  Jenny kiss'd me.

To Celia

BEN JONSON

Drink to me only with thine eyes,
  And I will pledge with mine;
Or leave a kiss but in the cup
  And I'll not look for wine.
The thirst that from the soul doth rise
  Doth ask a drink divine;
But might I of Jove's nectar sup,
  I would not change for thine.
I sent thee late a rosy wreath,
  Not so much honouring thee
As giving it a hope that there
  It could not wither'd be;
But thou thereon didst only breathe,
  And sent'st it back to me;
Since when it grows, and smells, I swear,
  Not of itself but thee!

Cards and Kisses

JOHN LYLY

Cupid and my Campaspe play'd
At cards for kisses—Cupid paid:
He stakes his quiver, bow, and arrows,
His mother's doves, and team of sparrows;
Loses them too; then down he throws
The coral of his lips, the rose
Growing on 's cheek (but none knows how);
With these, the crystal of his brow,
And then the dimple of his chin:
All these did my Campaspe win.
At last he set her both his eyes—
She won, and Cupid blind did rise.
  O Love! has she done this for thee?
  What shall, alas! become of me?

Rosaline

THOMAS LODGE

Like to the clear in highest sphere
  Where all imperial glory shines,
Of selfsame colour is her hair
  Whether unfolded or in twines:
    Heigh ho, fair Rosaline!
Her eyes are sapphires set in snow,
  Resembling heaven by every wink;
The gods do fear whenas they glow,
  And I do tremble when I think
    Heigh ho, would she were mine!
Her cheeks are like the blushing cloud
  That beautifies Aurora's face,
Or like the silver crimson shroud
  That Phoebus' smiling looks doth grace.
    Heigh ho, fair Rosaline!
Her lips are like two budded roses
  Whom ranks of lilies neighbour nigh,
Within whose bounds she balm encloses
  Apt to entice a deity:
    Heigh ho, would she were mine!
Her neck like to a stately tower
  Where Love himself imprison'd lies,
To watch for glances every hour
  From her divine and sacred eyes:
    Heigh ho, fair Rosaline!
Her paps are centres of delight,
  Her breasts are orbs of heavenly frame,
Where Nature moulds the dew of light
  To feed perfection with the same:
    Heigh ho, would she were mine!

With orient pearl, with ruby red,
   With marble white, with sapphire blue,
Her body every way is fed,
   Yet soft to touch and sweet in view:
      Heigh ho, fair Rosaline!
Nature herself her shape admires;
   The gods are wounded in her sight;
And Love forsakes his heavenly fires
   And at her eyes his brand doth light:
      Heigh ho, would she were mine!
Then muse not, Nymphs, though I bemoan
   The absence of fair Rosaline,
Since for a fair there's fairer none,
   Nor for her virtues so divine:
      Heigh ho, fair Rosaline!
Heigh ho, my heart! would God that she were mine!

To Amarantha;
That She Would Dishevel Her Hair

RICHARD LOVELACE

Amarantha sweet and fair,
Ah brade no more that shining hair!
As my curious hand or eye,
Hovering round thee, let it fly.

Let it fly as unconfin'd
As its calme ravisher, the wind,
Who hath left his darling, th'East,
To wanton o'er that spicie nest.

Ev'ry tress must be confest:
But neatly tangled at the best;
Like a clue of golden thread,
Most excellently ravelled.

Do not then wind up that light
In ribands, and o'er-cloud in night,
Like the sun in's early ray;
But shake your head, and scatter day.

See, 'tis broke! within this grove,
The bower and the walks of love,
Weary lie we downe and rest,
And fan each other's panting breast.

Here we'll strip and cool our fire,
In cream below, in milk-baths higher:
And when all wells are drawn dry,
I'll drink a tear out of thine eye.

Which our very joys shall leave,
That sorrows thus we can deceive;
Or our very sorrows weep,
That joys so ripe so little keep.

To Lucasta, Going to the Wars

RICHARD LOVELACE

Tell me not, Sweet, I am unkind,
  That from the nunnery
Of thy chaste breast and quiet mind
  To war and arms I fly.
True, a new mistress now I chase,
  The first foe in the field;
And with a stronger faith embrace
  A sword, a horse, a shield.
Yet this inconstancy is such
  As thou too shalt adore;
I could not love thee, Dear, so much,
  Loved I not Honour more.

The Scrutiny

RICHARD LOVELACE

Why should you swear I am forsworn,
Since thine I vowed to be?
Lady, it is already morn,
And 'twas last night I swore to thee
That fond impossibility.

Have I not loved thee much and long,
A tedious twelve hours' space?
I must all other beauties wrong,
And rob thee of a new embrace,
Could I still dote upon thy face.

Not but all joy in thy brown hair
By others may be found;—
But I must search the black and fair,
Like skilful mineralists that sound
For treasure in unploughed-up ground.

Then if, when I have loved my round,
Thou prov'st the pleasant she,
With spoils of meaner beauties crowned
I laden will return to thee,
Ev'n sated with variety.

Love Unkind

ISABEL ECCLESTONE MACKAY

Out upon the bleak hillside, the bleak hillside, he lay—
Her lips were red, and red the stream that slipped his life away.
Ah, crimson, crimson were her lips, but his were turning gray.
The troubled sky seemed bending low, bending low to hide
The foam-white face so wild upturned from off the bleak hillside—
White as the beaten foam her face, and she was wond'rous eyed.
The soft, south-wind came creeping up, creeping stealthily
To breathe upon his clay-cold face—but all too cold was he,
Too cold for you to warm, south-wind, since cold at heart was
    she!
Sweet morning peeped above the hill, above the hill to find
The shattered, useless, godlike thing the night had left behind—
Wept the sweet morn her crystal tears that love should prove
    unkind!

The Passionate Shepherd to His Love*

CHRISTOPHER MARLOWE

Come live with me and be my Love,
And we will all the pleasures prove
That hills and valleys, dales and fields,
Or woods or steepy mountain yields.
And we will sit upon the rocks,
And see the shepherds feed their flocks
By shallow rivers, to whose falls
Melodious birds sing madrigals.
And I will make thee beds of roses
And a thousand fragrant posies;
A cap of flowers, and a kirtle
Embroider'd all with leaves of myrtle.
A gown made of the finest wool
Which from our pretty lambs we pull;
Fair-lined slippers for the cold,
With buckles of the purest gold.
A belt of straw and ivy-buds
With coral clasps and amber studs:
And if these pleasures may thee move,
Come live with me and be my Love.
The shepherd swains shall dance and sing
For thy delight each May morning:
If these delights thy mind may move,
Then live with me and be my Love.

---

* See p. 73 for the nymph's reply.

To His Coy Mistress

ANDREW MARVELL

Had we but world enough, and time,
This coyness, lady, were no crime.
We would sit down and think which way
To walk, and pass our long love's day;
Thou by the Indian Ganges' side
Shouldst rubies find; I by the tide
Of Humber would complain. I would
Love you ten years before the Flood;
And you should, if you please, refuse
Till the conversion of the Jews.
My vegetable love should grow
Vaster than empires, and more slow.
An hundred years should go to praise
Thine eyes, and on thy forehead gaze;
Two hundred to adore each breast,
But thirty thousand to the rest;
An age at least to every part,
And the last age should show your heart.
For, lady, you deserve this state,
Nor would I love at lower rate.

But at my back I always hear
Time's winged chariot hurrying near;
And yonder all before us lie
Deserts of vast eternity.
Thy beauty shall no more be found,
Nor, in thy marble vault, shall sound
My echoing song; then worms shall try
That long preserv'd virginity,
And your quaint honour turn to dust,
And into ashes all my lust.
The grave's a fine and private place,
But none I think do there embrace.

Now therefore, while the youthful hue
Sits on thy skin like morning dew,
And while thy willing soul transpires
At every pore with instant fires,
Now let us sport us while we may;
And now, like am'rous birds of prey,
Rather at once our time devour,
Than languish in his slow-chapp'd power.
Let us roll all our strength, and all
Our sweetness, up into one ball;
And tear our pleasures with rough strife
Through the iron gates of life.
Thus, though we cannot make our sun
Stand still, yet we will make him run.

I'll Never Love Thee More

JAMES GRAHAM, MARQUIS OF MONTROSE

My dear and only Love, I pray
  That little world of thee
Be govern'd by no other sway
  Than purest monarchy;
For if confusion have a part
  (Which virtuous souls abhor),
And hold a synod in thine heart,
  I'll never love thee more.

Like Alexander I will reign,
  And I will reign alone;
My thoughts did evermore disdain
  A rival on my throne.
He either fears his fate too much,
  Or his deserts are small,
That dares not put it to the touch,
  To gain or lose it all.

And in the empire of thine heart,
  Where I should solely be,
If others do pretend a part
  Or dare to vie with me,
Or if Committees thou erect,
  And go on such a score,
I'll laugh and sing at thy neglect,
  And never love thee more.

But if thou wilt prove faithful then,
   And constant of thy word,
I'll make thee glorious by my pen
   And famous by my sword;
I'll serve thee in such noble ways
   Was never heard before;
I'll crown and deck thee all with bays,
   And love thee more and more.

Beauty Bathing

ANTHONY MUNDAY

Beauty sat bathing by a spring,
  Where fairest shades did hide her;
The winds blew calm, the birds did sing,
  The cool streams ran beside her.
My wanton thoughts enticed mine eye
  To see what was forbidden:
But better memory said Fie;
  So vain desire was chidden—
    Hey nonny nonny O!
    Hey nonny nonny!
Into a slumber then I fell,
  And fond imagination
Seemed to see, but could not tell,
  Her feature or her fashion:
But ev'n as babes in dreams do smile,
  And sometimes fall a-weeping,
So I awaked as wise that while
  As when I fell a-sleeping.

I Do Not Love Thee

CAROLINE NORTON

I do not love thee!—no! I do not love thee!
And yet when thou art absent I am sad;
  And envy even the bright blue sky above thee,
Whose quiet stars may see thee and be glad.

I do not love thee!—yet, I know not why,
Whate'er thou dost seems still well done, to me:
  And often in my solitude I sigh
That those I do love are not more like thee!

I do not love thee!—yet, when thou art gone,
I hate the sound (though those who speak be dear)
  Which breaks the lingering echo of the tone
Thy voice of music leaves upon my ear.

I do not love thee!—yet thy speaking eyes,
With their deep, bright, and most expressive blue,
  Between me and the midnight heaven arise,
Oftener than any eyes I ever knew.

I know I do not love thee! yet, alas!
Others will scarcely trust my candid heart;
  And oft I catch them smiling as they pass,
Because they see me gazing where thou art.

Rondel

CHARLES D'ORLEANS

Strengthen, my Love, this castle of my heart,
And with some store of pleasure give me aid,
For Jealousy, with all them of his part,
Strong siege about the weary tower has laid.
Nay, if to break his bands thou art afraid,
Too weak to make his cruel force depart,
Strengthen at least this castle of my heart,
And with some store of pleasure give me aid.
Nay, let not Jealousy, for all his art
Be master, and the tower in ruin laid,
That still, ah Love! thy gracious rule obeyed.
Advance, and give me succour of thy part;
Strengthen, my Love, this castle of my heart.

A Love Symphony

A. W. E. O'SHAUGHNESSY

Along the garden ways just now
I heard the flowers speak;
The white rose told me of your brow,
The red rose of your cheek;
The lily of your bended head,
The bindweed of your hair:
Each looked its loveliest and said
You were more fair.

I went into the wood anon,
And heard the wild birds sing
How sweet you were; they warbled on,
Piped, trilled the self-same thing.
Thrush, blackbird, linnet, without pause,
The burden did repeat,
And still began again because
You were more sweet.

And then I went down to the sea,
And heard it murmuring too,
Part of an ancient mystery,
All made of me and you.
How many a thousand years ago
I loved, and you were sweet—
Longer I could not stay, and so
I fled back to your feet.

The Enchantment

THOMAS OTWAY

I did but look and love awhile,
 'Twas but for one half-hour;
Then to resist I had no will,
 And now I have no power.

To sigh and wish is all my ease;
 Sighs which do heat impart
Enough to melt the coldest ice,
 Yet cannot warm your heart.

O would your pity give my heart
 One corner of your breast,
'Twould learn of yours the winning art,
 And quickly steal the rest.

What Cunning Can Express

EDWARD DE VERE, EARL OF OXFORD

What cunning can express
The favor of her face
To whom in this distress
I do appeal for grace?
A thousand Cupids fly
About her gentle eye.

From whence each throws a dart
That kindleth soft sweet fire
Within my sighing heart,
Possessèd by desire.
No sweeter life I try
Than in her love to die.

The lily in the field
That glories in his white,
For pureness now must yield
And render up his right.
Heaven pictured in her face
Doth promise joy and grace.

Fair Cynthia's silver light
That beats on running streams
Compares not with her white,
Whose hairs are all sunbeams.
Her virtues so do shine
As day unto mine eyne.

With this there is a red
Exceeds the damask rose,
Which in her cheeks is spread,
Whence every favor grows.
In sky there is no star
That she surmounts not far.

When Phoebus from the bed
Of Thetis doth arise,
The morning blushing red
In fair carnation wise,
He shows it in her face
As queen of every grace.

This pleasant lily-white,
This taint of roseate red,
This Cynthia's silver light,
This sweet fair Dea spread,
These sunbeams in mine eye,
These beauties make me die!

Love and Age

THOMAS LOVE PEACOCK

I play'd with you 'mid cowslips blowing,
   When I was six and you were four;
When garlands weaving, flower-balls throwing,
   Were pleasures soon to please no more.
Through groves and meads, o'er grass and heather,
   With little playmates, to and fro,
We wander'd hand in hand together;
   But that was sixty years ago.

You grew a lovely roseate maiden,
   And still our early love was strong;
Still with no care our days were laden,
   They glided joyously along;
And I did love you very dearly,
   How dearly words want power to show;
I thought your heart was touch'd as nearly;
   But that was fifty years ago.

Then other lovers came around you,
   Your beauty grew from year to year,
And many a splendid circle found you
   The centre of its glimmering sphere.
I saw you then, first vows forsaking,
   On rank and wealth your hand bestow;
O, then I thought my heart was breaking!—
   But that was forty years ago.

And I lived on, to wed another:
　No cause she gave me to repine;
And when I heard you were a mother,
　I did not wish the children mine.
My own young flock, in fair progression,
　Made up a pleasant Christmas row:
My joy in them was past expression;
　But that was thirty years ago.

You grew a matron plump and comely,
　You dwelt in fashion's brightest blaze;
My earthly lot was far more homely;
　But I too had my festal days.
No merrier eyes have ever glisten'd
　Around the hearth-stone's wintry glow,
Than when my youngest child was christen'd;
　But that was twenty years ago.

Time pass'd. My eldest girl was married,
　And I am now a grandsire gray;
One pet of four years old I've carried
　Among the wild-flower'd meads to play.
In our old fields of childish pleasure,
　Where now, as then, the cowslips blow,
She fills her basket's ample measure;
　And that is not ten years ago.

But though first love's impassion'd blindness
　Has pass'd away in colder light,
I still have thought of you with kindness,
　And shall do, till our last good-night.
The ever-rolling silent hours
　Will bring a time we shall not know,
When our young days of gathering flowers
　Will be an hundred years ago.

Phillida and Coridon

NICHOLAS BRETON

In the merry month of May,
In a morn by break of day,
Forth I walk'd by the wood-side
When as May was in his pride:
There I spied all alone
Phillida and Coridon.
Much ado there was, God wot!
He would love and she would not.
She said, Never man was true;
He said, None was false to you.
He said, He had loved her long;
She said, Love should have no wrong.
Coridon would kiss her then;
She said, Maids must kiss no men
Till they did for good and all;
Then she made the shepherd call
All the heavens to witness truth
Never loved a truer youth.
Thus with many a pretty oath,
Yea and nay, and faith and troth,
Such as silly shepherds use
When they will not Love abuse,
Love, which had been long deluded,
Was with kisses sweet concluded;
And Phillida, with garlands gay,
Was made the Lady of the May.

The Nymph's Reply to the Shepherd

SIR WALTER RALEIGH

If all the world and love were young,
And truth in every shepherd's tongue,
These pretty pleasures might me move
To live with thee and be thy love.

Time drives the flocks from field to fold,
When rivers rage and rocks grow cold;
And Philomel becometh dumb;
The rest complains of cares to come.

The flowers do fade, and wanton fields
To wayward winter reckoning yields:
A honey tongue, a heart of gall,
Is fancy's spring, but sorrow's fall.

The gowns, thy shoes, thy beds of roses,
Thy cap, thy kirtle, and thy posies
Soon break, soon wither, soon forgotten,—
In folly ripe, in reason rotten.

Thy belt of straw and ivy buds,
Thy coral clasps and amber studs,
All these in me no means can move
To come to thee and be thy love.

But could youth last and love still breed,
Had joys no date nor age no need,
Then these delights my mind might move
To live with thee and be thy love.

* See p. 58

The Ripest Peach

JAMES WHITCOMB RILEY

The ripest peach is highest on the tree—
And so her love, beyond the reach of me,
Is dearest in my sight. Sweet breezes, bow
Her heart down to me where I worship now!

She looms aloft where every eye may see
The ripest peach is highest on the tree.
Such fruitage as her love I know, alas!
I may not reach here from the orchard grass.

I drink the sunshine showered past her lips
As roses drain the dewdrop as it drips.
The ripest peach is highest on the tree,
And so mine eyes gaze upward eagerly.

Why—why do I not turn away in wrath
And pluck some heart here hanging in my path?—
Love's lower boughs bend with them—but, ah me!
The ripest peach is highest on the tree!

A Song of a Young Lady to Her Ancient Lover

JOHN WILMOT, EARL OF ROCHESTER

Ancient Person, for whom I
All the flattering youth defy,
Long be it e'er thou grow old,
Aching, shaking, crazy cold;
But still continue as thou art,
Ancient Person of my heart.

On thy withered lips and dry,
Which like barren furrows lie,
Brooding kisses I will pour,
Shall thy youthful heart restore,
Such kind show'rs in autumn fall,
And a second spring recall;
Nor from thee will ever part,
Ancient Person of my heart.

Thy nobler parts, which but to name
In our sex would be counted shame,
By ages frozen grasp possest,
From their ice shall be released,
And, soothed by my reviving hand,
In former warmth and vigour stand.
All a lover's wish can reach,
For thy joy my love shall teach;
And for thy pleasure shall improve
All that art can add to love.
Yet still I love thee without art,
Ancient Person of my heart.

Love from the North

CHRISTINA ROSSETTI

I had a love in soft south land,
  Beloved through April far in May;
He waited on my lightest breath,
  And never dared to say me nay.

He saddened if my cheer was sad,
  But gay he grew if I was gay;
We never differed on a hair,
  My yes his yes, my nay his nay.

The wedding hour was come, the aisles
  Were flushed with sun and flowers that day;
I pacing balanced in my thoughts,—
  'It's quite too late to think of nay.'—

My bridegroom answered in his turn,
  Myself had almost answered 'yea':
When through the flashing nave I heard.
  A struggle and resounding 'nay.'

Bridemaids and bridegroom shrank in fear,
  But I stood high who stood at bay:
'And if I answer yea, fair Sir,
  What man art thou to bar with nay?'

He was a strong man from the north,
  Light-locked, with eyes of dangerous gray:
'Put yea by for another time
  In which I will not say thee nay.'

He took me in his strong white arms,
  He bore me on his horse away
O'er crag, morass, and hair-breadth pass,
  But never asked me yea or nay.

He made me fast with book and bell,
  With links of love he makes me stay;
Till now I've neither heart nor power
  Nor will nor wish to say him nay.

Phyllis is My Only Joy

SIR CHARLES SEDLEY

Phyllis is my only joy,
  Faithless as the winds or seas;
Sometimes coming, sometimes coy,
  Yet she never fails to please;
If with a frown
I am cast down,
Phyllis smiling,
And beguiling,
Makes me happier than before.

Though, alas! too late I find
  Nothing can her fancy fix,
Yet the moment she is kind
  I forgive her all her tricks;
Which, though I see,
I can't get free;
She deceiving,
I believing;
What need lovers wish for more?

To Celia

SIR CHARLES SEDLEY

Not, Celia, that I juster am
  Or better than the rest!
For I would change each hour, like them,
  Were not my heart at rest.

But I am tied to very thee
  By every thought I have;
Thy face I only care to see,
  Thy heart I only crave.

All that in woman is adored
  In thy dear self I find—
For the whole sex can but afford
  The handsome and the kind.

Why then should I seek further store,
  And still make love anew?
When change itself can give no more,
  'Tis easy to be true!

Sonnet XVIII

WILLIAM SHAKESPEARE

Shall I compare thee to a Summer's day?
Thou art more lovely and more temperate:
Rough winds do shake the darling buds of May,
And Summer's lease hath all too short a date:
Sometime too hot the eye of heaven shines,
And often is his gold complexion dimm'd;
And every fair from fair sometime declines,
By chance or nature's changing course untrimm'd:
But thy eternal Summer shall not fade
Nor lose possession of that fair thou owest;
Nor shall Death brag thou wanderest in his shade,
When in eternal lines to time thou growest:
  So long as men can breathe, or eyes can see,
  So long lives this, and this gives life to thee.

Sonnet LVII

WILLIAM SHAKESPEARE

Being your slave, what should I do but tend
Upon the hours and times of your desire?
I have no precious time at all to spend,
Nor services to do, till you require.
Nor dare I chide the world-without-end hour
Whilst I, my sovereign, watch the clock for you,
Nor think the bitterness of absence sour
When you have bid your servant once adieu;
Nor dare I question with my jealous thought
Where you may be, or your affairs suppose,
But, like a sad slave, stay and think of nought
Save, where you are how happy you make those!
  So true a fool is love, that in your Will,
  Though you do any thing, he thinks no ill.

Sonnet LXXV

WILLIAM SHAKESPEARE

So are you to my thoughts as food to life,
Or as sweet-season'd showers are to the ground;
And for the peace of you I hold such strife
As 'twixt a miser and his wealth is found.
Now proud as an enjoyer, and anon
Doubting the filching age will steal his treasure;
Now counting best to be with you alone,
Then better'd that the world may see my pleasure:
Sometime all full with feasting on your sight,
And by and by clean starved for a look;
Possessing or pursuing no delight,
Save what is had, or must from you be took.
  Thus do I pine and surfeit day by day,
  Or gluttoning on all, or all away.

Sonnet CXXX

WILLIAM SHAKESPEARE

My mistress' eyes are nothing like the sun;
Coral is far more red than her lips' red;
If snow be white, why then her breasts are dun;
If hairs be wires, black wires grow on her head.
I have seen roses damasked, red and white,
But no such roses see I in her cheeks;
And in some perfumes is there more delight
Than in the breath that from my mistress reeks.
I love to hear her speak, yet well I know
That music hath a far more pleasing sound;
I grant I never saw a goddess go;
My mistress when she walks treads on the ground.
  And yet, by heaven, I think my love as rare
  As any she belied with false compare.

Sonnet XCI

WILLIAM SHAKESPEARE

Some glory in their birth, some in their skill,
Some in their wealth, some in their body's force,
Some in their garments though new-fangled ill;
Some in their hawks and hounds, some in their horse;
And every humour hath his adjunct pleasure,
Wherein it finds a joy above the rest:
But these particulars are not my measure,
All these I better in one general best.
Thy love is better than high birth to me,
Richer than wealth, prouder than garments' costs,
Of more delight than hawks and horses be;
And having thee, of all men's pride I boast:
  Wretched in this alone, that thou mayst take
  All this away, and me most wretched make.

Sonnet CXLI

WILLIAM SHAKESPEARE

In faith, I do not love thee with mine eyes,
For they in thee a thousand errors note;
But 'tis my heart that loves what they despise,
Who in despite of view is pleased to dote.
Nor are mine ears with thy tongue's tune delighted,
Nor tender feeling to base touches prone,
Nor taste, nor smell, desire to be invited
To any sensual feast with thee alone;
But my five wits, nor my five senses can
Dissuade one foolish heart from serving thee,
Who leaves unswayed the likeness of a man,
Thy proud heart's slave and vassal wretch to be.
  Only my plague thus far I count my gain,
  That she that makes me sin awards me pain.

The Indian Serenade

PERCY BYSSHE SHELLEY

I arise from dreams of thee
  In the first sweet sleep of night,
When the winds are breathing low,
  And the stars are shining bright.
I arise from dreams of thee,
  And a spirit in my feet
Hath led me—who knows how?
  To thy chamber window, Sweet!

The wandering airs they faint
  On the dark, the silent stream—
And the champak's odours fall
  Like sweet thoughts in a dream;
The nightingale's complaint,
  It dies upon her heart,
As I must on thine,
  O beloved as thou art!

O lift me from the grass!
  I die! I faint! I fail!
Let thy love in kisses rain
  On my lips and eyelids pale.
My cheek is cold and white, alas!
  My heart beats loud and fast:
O press it to thine own again,
  Where it will break at last!

Love's Arithmetic

SIR EDWARD SHERBURNE

By a gentle river laid,
Thirsis to his Phillis said,
'Equal to these sandy grains,
Is the number of my pains:
And the drops within their bounds
Speak the sum of all my wounds.'

Phillis, who like passion burns,
Thirsis answer thus returns:
'Many, as the Earth hath leaves,
Are the griefs my heart receives;
And the stars, which Heaven inspires,
Reckon my consuming fires.'

Then the shepherd, in the pride
Of his happy love, replied:
'With the choristers of air
Shall our numerous joys compare;
And our mutual pleasures vie
With the Cupids in thine eye.'

Thus the willing shepherdess
Did her ready love express:
'In delights our pains shall cease,
And our war be cur'd by peace;
We shall count our griefs with blisses,
Thousand torments, thousand kisses.'

Had I a Heart for Falsehood Framed

RICHARD BRINSLEY SHERIDAN

Had I a heart for falsehood framed,
I ne'er could injure you;
For though your tongue no promise claimed,
  Your charms would make me true:
To you no soul shall bear deceit,
  No stranger offer wrong;
But friends in all the aged you'll meet,
  And lovers in the young.

For when they learn that you have blest
  Another with your heart,
They'll bid aspiring passion rest,
  And act a brother's part;
Then, lady, dread not here deceit,
  Nor fear to suffer wrong;
For friends in all the aged you'll meet,
  And lovers in the young.

Cupid, Because Thou

SIR PHILIP SIDNEY

Cupid, because thou shin'st in Stella's eyes,
That from her locks, thy day-nets, no scapes free,
That those lips swell, so full of thee they be,
That her sweet breath makes oft thy flames to rise,

That in her breast thy pap well sugared lies,
That her Grace gracious makes thy wrongs, that she,
What words soe'er she speak persuades for thee,
That her clear voice lifts thy fame to the skies:

Thou countest Stella thine, like those whose powers
Having got up a breach by fighting well,
Cry, 'Victory, this fair day all is ours.'

Oh no, her heart is such a citadel,
So fortified with wit, stored with disdain,
That to win it, is all the skill and pain.

I Prithee Send Me Back My Heart

SIR JOHN SUCKLING

I prithee send me back my heart,
Since I cannot have thine;
For if from yours you will not part,
Why then shouldst thou have mine?

Yet now I think on't, let it lie,
To find it were in vain;
For th'hast a thief in either eye
Would steal it back again.

Why should two hearts in one breast lie,
And yet not lodge together?
O love, where is thy sympathy,
If thus our breasts thou sever?

But love is such a mystery,
I cannot find it out;
For when I think I'm best resolved,
I then am most in doubt.

Then farewell care, and farewell woe,
I will no longer pine;
For I'll believe I have her heart
As much as she hath mine.

Out Upon It, I Have Lov'd

SIR JOHN SUCKLING

Out upon it, I have lov'd
Three whole days together;
And am like to love three more,
If it prove fair weather.

Time shall moult away his wings,
Ere he shall discover
In the whole wide world again
Such a constant lover.

But the spite on't is, no praise
Is due at all to me;
Love with me had made no stays,
Had it any been but she.

Had it any been but she,
And that very face,
There had been at least ere this
A dozen dozen in her place.

When, Dearest, I but Think of Thee

SIR JOHN SUCKLING

When, dearest, I but think of thee,
Methinks all things that lovely be
  Are present, and my soul delighted:
For beauties that from worth arise
Are like the grace of deities,
  Still present with us, tho' unsighted.

Thus while I sit and sigh the day
With all his borrow'd lights away,
  Till night's black wings do overtake me,
Thinking on thee, thy beauties then,
As sudden lights do sleepy men,
  So they by their bright rays awake me.

Thus absence dies, and dying proves
No absence can subsist with loves
  That do partake of fair perfection:
Since in the darkest night they may
By love's quick motion find a way
  To see each other by reflection.

The waving sea can with each flood
Bathe some high promont that hath stood
  Far from the main up in the river:
O think not then but love can do
As much! for that's an ocean too,
  Which flows not every day, but ever!

Tides

SARA TEASDALE

Love in my heart was a fresh tide flowing
Where the starlike sea gulls soar;
The sun was keen and the foam was blowing
High on the rocky shore.

But now in the dusk the tide is turning,
Lower the sea gulls soar,
And the waves that rose in resistless yearning
Are broken forevermore.

Arbor Amoris

FRANÇOIS VILLON

I have a tree, a graft of Love,
That in my heart has taken root;
Sad are the buds and blooms thereof,
And bitter sorrow is its fruit;
Yet, since it was a tender shoot,
So greatly hath its shadow spread,
That underneath all joy is dead,
And all my pleasant days are flown,
Nor can I slay it, nor instead
Plant any tree, save this alone.
Ah, yet, for long and long enough
My tears were rain about its root,
And though the fruit be harsh thereof,
I scarcely looked for better fruit
Than this, that carefully I put
In garner, for the bitter bread
Whereon my weary life is fed:
Ah, better were the soil unsown
That bears such growths; but Love instead
Will plant no tree, but this alone.
Ah, would that this new spring, whereof
The leaves and flowers flush into shoot,
I might have succour and aid of Love,
To prune these branches at the root,
That long have borne such bitter fruit,
And graft a new bough, comforted
With happy blossoms white and red;
So pleasure should for pain atone,
Nor Love slay this tree, nor instead
Plant any tree, but this alone.

L'ENVOY

Princess, by whom my hope is fed,
My heart thee prays in lowlihead
To prune the ill boughs overgrown,
Nor slay Love's tree, nor plant instead
Another tree, save this alone.

Go, Lovely Rose

EDMUND WALLER

Go, lovely Rose—
Tell her that wastes her time and me,
  That now she knows,
When I resemble her to thee,
How sweet and fair she seems to be.

  Tell her that's young,
And shuns to have her graces spied,
  That hadst thou sprung
In deserts where no men abide,
Thou must have uncommended died.

  Small is the worth
Of beauty from the light retired:
  Bid her come forth,
Suffer herself to be desired,
And not blush so to be admired.

  Then die—that she
The common fate of all things rare
  May read in thee;
How small a part of time they share
That are so wondrous sweet and fair!

To Phyllis

EDMUND WALLER

Phyllis! why should we delay
Pleasures shorter than the day?
Can we (which we never can)
Stretch our lives beyond their span,
Beauty like a shadow flies,
And our youth before us dies.
Or, would youth and beauty stay,
Love has wings, and will away.
Love has swifter wings than Time;
Change in love to heaven doth climb.
Gods, that never change their state,
Vary oft their love and hate.
Phyllis! to this truth we owe
All the love betwixt us two.
Let not you and I inquire
What has been our past desire;
On what shepherds you have smiled,
Or what nymphs I have beguiled;
Leave it to the planets too,
What we shall hereafter do;
For the joys we now may prove,
Take advice of present love.

The Self Banished

EDMUND WALLER

It is not that I love you less
Than when before your feet I lay,
But to prevent the sad increase
Of hopeless love, I keep away.

In vain (alas!) for everything
Which I have known belong to you,
Your form does to my fancy bring,
And makes my old wounds bleed anew.

Who in the spring from the new sun
Already has a fever got,
Too late begins those shafts to shun,
Which Phœbus through his veins has shot.

Too late he would the pain assuage,
And to thick shadows does retire;
About with him he bears the rage,
And in his tainted blood the fire.

But vow'd I have, and never must
Your banish'd servant trouble you;
For if I break, you may distrust
The vow I made to love you, too.

Against Indifference

CHARLES WEBBE

More love or more disdain I crave;
 Sweet, be not still indifferent:
O send me quickly to my grave,
 Or else afford me more content!
Or love or hate me more or less,
For love abhors all lukewarmness.

Give me a tempest if 'twill drive
 Me to the place where I would be;
Or if you'll have me still alive,
 Confess you will be kind to me.
Give hopes of bliss or dig my grave:
More love or more disdain I crave.

The Je Ne Scai Quoi

WILLIAM WHITEHEAD

Yes, I'm in love, I feel it now,
And Cælia has undone me;
And yet I'll swear I can't tell how
The pleasing plague stole on me.

'Tis not her face that love creates,
For there no graces revel;
'Tis not her shape, for there the fates
Have rather been uncivil.

'Tis not her air, for sure in that
There's nothing more than common;
And all her sense is only chat
Like any other woman.

Her voice, her touch, might give th'alarm—
'Twas both perhaps, or neither;
In short, 'twas that provoking charm
Of Cælia altogether.

I Loved a Lass

GEORGE WITHER

I loved a lass, a fair one,
   As fair as e'er was seen;
She was indeed a rare one,
   Another Sheba Queen:
But, fool as then I was,
   I thought she loved me too:
But now, alas! she's left me,
   Falero, lero, loo!

Her hair like gold did glister,
   Each eye was like a star,
She did surpass her sister,
   Which pass'd all others far;
She would me honey call,
   She'd—O she'd kiss me too!
But now, alas! she's left me,
   Falero, lero, loo!

Many a merry meeting
   My love and I have had;
She was my only sweeting,
   She made my heart full glad;
The tears stood in her eyes
   Like to the morning dew:
But now, alas! she's left me,
   Falero, lero, loo!

Her cheeks were like the cherry,
  Her skin was white as snow;
When she was blithe and merry
  She angel-like did show;
Her waist exceeding small,
  The fives did fit her shoe:
But now, alas! she's left me,
  Falero, lero, loo!

In summer time or winter
  She had her heart's desire;
I still did scorn to stint her
  From sugar, sack, or fire;
The world went round about,
  No cares we ever knew:
But now, alas! she's left me,
  Falero, lero, loo!

To maidens' vows and swearing
  Henceforth no credit give;
You may give them the hearing,
  But never them believe;
They are as false as fair,
  Unconstant, frail, untrue:
For mine, alas! hath left me,
  Falero, lero, loo!

A Complaint

WILLIAM WORDSWORTH

There is a change—and I am poor;
Your love hath been, nor long ago,
A fountain at my fond heart's door,
Whose only business was to flow;
And flow it did; not taking heed
Of its own bounty, or my need.

What happy moments did I count!
Blest was I then all bliss above!
Now, for that consecrated fount
Of murmuring, sparkling, living love,
What have I? Shall I dare to tell?
A comfortless and hidden well.

A well of love—it may be deep—
I trust it is,—and never dry:
What matter? If the waters sleep
In silence and obscurity.
—Such change, and at the very door
Of my fond heart, hath made me poor.

Rondeau

SIR THOMAS WYATT

For to love her for her looks lovely
   My heart was set in thought right firmly,
   Trusting by truth to have had redress;
   But she hath made another promise,
   And hath given me leave full honestly.

   Yet do I not rejoice it greatly,
   For on my faith I loved too surely:
   But reason will that I do cease
      For to love her.

Since that in love the pain's been deadly,
   Me think it best that readily
   I do return to my first address;
   For at this time too great is the press
   And perils appear too abundantly
      For to love her.

Sonnet

SIR THOMAS WYATT

The long love that in my thought doth harbour
  And in my heart doth keep his residence
  Into my face presseth with bold pretence
  And therein campeth spreading his banner.
She that me learneth to love and suffer
  And wills that my trust and lust's negligence
  Be reined by reason, shame, and reverence
  With his hardiness taketh displeasure.
Where with all unto the heart's forest he fleeeth
  Leaving his enterprise with pain and cry,
  And there him hideth and not appeareth.
What may I do when my master feareth?
  But in the field with him to live and die?
  For good is the life, ending faithfully.

Index of First Lines

Along the garden ways just now   66
Amarantha sweet and fair   53
Ancient Person, for whom I   75
Ask me, Lesbia, what the sum delightful   27
Beauty clear and fair   40
Beauty sat bathing by a spring   63
Being your slave, what should I do but tend   81
Bid me to live, and I will live   44
Busy old fool, unruly Sun   30
By a gentle river laid   87
Come live with me and be my Love   58
Cupid and my Campaspe play'd   50
Cupid, because thou shin'st in Stella's eyes   89
Drink to me only with thine eyes   49
Flattering Hope, away and leave me   12
For her gait, if she be walking   18
For to love her for her looks lovely   104
Go fetch to me a pint o' wine   21
Go, lovely Rose—   96
Had I a heart for falsehood framed   88
Had we but world enough, and time   59
He that loves a rosy cheek   26
Her eyes the glow-worm lend thee   45
How do I love thee? Let me count the ways   19
How many paltry foolish painted things   36
I am two fools, I know   34
I arise from dreams of thee   86
I dare not ask a kiss   46
I did but look and love awhile   67
I do not love thee!—no! I do not love thee!   64
I dreamt I was in love again   15
I had a love in soft south land   76

I have a tree, a graft of Love   94
I loved a lass, a fair one   101
I play'd with you 'mid cowslips blowing   70
I pray thee, leave, love me no more   35
I prithee send me back my heart   90
I wonder by my troth, what thou and I   29
If all the world and love were young   73
In faith, I do not love thee with mine eyes   85
In the merry month of May   72
It is not that I love you less   98
It is not, Celia, in our power   39
It was not in the Winter   47
Jenny kiss'd me when we met   48
Like to the clear in highest sphere   51
Love in fantastic triumph sate   14
Love in my heart was a fresh tide flowing   93
Love is the blossom where there blows   41
More love or more disdain I crave   99
My dear and only Love, I pray   61
My mistress' eyes are nothing like the sun   83
Not, Celia, that I juster am   79
O my Luve's like a red, red rose   22
Out upon it, I have lov'd   91
Out upon the bleak hillside, the bleak hillside, he lay   57
Phyllis is my only joy   78
Phyllis! why should we delay   97
Room after room   20
Shall I compare thee to a Summer's day?   80
She walks in Beauty, like the night   24
So are you to my thoughts as food to life   82
Some glory in their birth, some in their skill   84
So shuts the marigold her leaves   17
So we'll go no more a-roving   23
Strengthen, my Love, this castle of my heart   65

Sweetest love, I do not go   32
Tell me not, Sweet, I am unkind   55
The light winds on the streamers play   10
The long love that in my thought doth harbour   105
The ripest peach is highest on the tree   74
There is a change—and I am poor   103
There is a garden in her face   25
There is a Lady sweet and kind   7
To plead my faith where faith had no reward   38
What cunning can express   68
When, dearest, I but think of thee   92
Why do I love? go ask the glorious sun   37
'Why do I love' You, Sir?   28
Why should you swear I am forsworn   56
Why, my heart, do we love her so?   43
Yes, I'm in love, I feel it now   100
Your lines poetic, Sir, I read   8

*Typeset in the United Kingdom
by Tiger of the Stripe in
Adobe Garamond Premier Pro
Using Adobe InDesign*

♥

www.ingramcontent.com/pod-product-compliance
Lightning Source LLC
Chambersburg PA
CBHW020013050426
42450CB00005B/443